# And the life she brings . . .

Karanjodh Singh

**WRITERS REPUBLIC L.L.C.**
515 Summit Ave. Unit R1
Union City, NJ 07087, USA

**Website:** *www.writersrepublic.com*
**Hotline:** *1-877-656-6838*
**Email:** *info@writersrepublic.com*

Ordering Information:
Quantity sales. Special discounts are available on quantity purchases by corporations, associations, and others. For details, contact the publisher at the address above.

Library of Congress Control Number:     2020926001
ISBN-13:          978-1-63728-118-5     [Paperback Edition]
                  978-1-63728-119-2     [Digital Edition]

Rev. date: 01/07/2021

*Certainly for mom and my sisters.*

And the life she brings with the boomerangs that she makes.

I don't know if I should thank her mother
more or god because they both have
built her breathtakingly beautiful.

Though all girls are sunshine but she
flickers different.

The only chaos I want to be in is to have her eyes on little her so I won't be able to tell which ones are more beautiful, mother's or daughter's?

If magic is real then she's the living proof of it.

# Goddess

And she's the reason I believe that god
must be a woman

All the colognes of the world at one side and
there she goes with her fragrance of
Innocence.

And she becomes more mellow as the days are passing by,

She's got something to wonder, god, to wonder in her eyes.

Naked minds make more love than naked bodies could ever be.

And I believe all the girls carry poetry, you just gotta look behind that flesh and bones.

Her eyes have been keeping stars but her heart, oh lord, her heart has been a home for the miracles.

Undress your thoughts darling, I love naked minds.

Damn! Her faith scares the hell out of the devil.

Darling, let's hold to the "now" for a while,
We'll talk about the "later" later.

And I've been wondering if imperfectly perfect is your last name? Is it?

Watch out when she shines as when she shines, she shines brighter than the Sirius.

I guess I am literally too sure that I'll love you forever.

But did she tell you that she alights the moon?

You may slow down her rain but you can't put down her thunder.

Take good care of her heart, you know, she's got dreams dancing at the window of her heart.

Find her in the places so young and wild.

His love for her conspicuously flickers in his eyes.

Worlds evolve when souls dissolve.

And sometimes, only sometimes, few days fade away the love of ages. Don't let them.

And when you're riding the wind,
make sure you don't keep your
eyes on the rear view mirror.

In a red dress and under the midnight moon, oh dear lord, she looked like happiness.

I wonder how she's got, Such courage, such flowers, Them thorns, them powers.

The bitter in her is the sweet that I've been looking for.

There's a hope in me still alive that I'll touch the stars that you keep hidden.

You smiled and I felt life, tell me just one thing, were we drunk?

She made me cross my limits and set it beyond my reach. All I see now is a freedom that follows me definitely.

The "crazy" that she has, people
die in search for that.

She made me see the happiness I carried over my shoulders when all of me was wandering just to borrow few smiles.

Give her all the love of the world but make sure you let her carry that she has for herself.

And we don't fall for touch, because our souls intertwine,
I believe it's all her now that I call mind of mine.

And her smile is my blanket in
my winter of troubles.

And the ocean danced at the rhythm of the waves when we kissed under the moonlight.

Kind,
Beautiful,
and sweet,
I guess life's too short to count all her
gorgeous colours

She's a goddess wearing
the halo of Kindness.

Why can't we just let our lovers go
and wait on our soulmates?

Her shiny hair felt like a sacred halo and twinkling eyes like a deep blue ocean, I guess I knew that I have chosen the poetry.

Life isn't about luxury cars, expensive shoes or big houses but it's all about buying groceries at the store with your family while your little one asks " daddy, why mommy's eyes are so beautiful?

If god reformed the universe again, I'd still search for only you in every corner.

Don't be so drenched in their light
that you almost forget your own.

They all kept praising her beauty and
I won her with my good intentions.

I want us to be an old couple with young souls in the wild streets of new York.

And I often wonder if she's the one who brings,
Spring to the trees,
Colour to the sky,
smile to the heaven,
Life to the souls,
I wonder if she does it, I often wonder.

Find the ones who turn all your monday
mornings into friday evenings.

How beautiful the word beautiful
gets when I call her beautiful.

Forget soulmate, you're my soul bride.

I wanna be with you until the sun gets cold, oceans become dry, horizon comes to an end. Wait, does it sound like forever?

Sort of love that lights up the places?
Our's.

I still tremble over the rush that
went through my veins when I
touched the fingertips of yours.

Hearts met so did the eyes, Stars
collapsed so did the skies.

Hold on to me like people hold
on to their grudges.

If only words could describe her
beauty I wonder how many poets
this world would have.

Everyday she plants new flowers of kindness in the garden of her soul.

And I found my twilight when everyone
else were waiting for stars to show up.

All she wants is your love to be fair,
Honest,
Filled with the care.

Give her smiles,
There are too many already out there to gift
her regrets.

She's a mother to my daughter,
A friend to my soul,
Rose to my thorns,
The missing piece of my whole.

The universe responds to her every single vibe that even a smirk of her never goes unnoticed.

Stop chasing beautiful. keep
them if they're kind.

# *Love*

It's in her eyes, that's where I first realised,
She holds love in them but tell me lies,
Its's in her eyes, beautiful, big and wide,
I can see it in her eyes,

It's in her lips,
when she looks at me, She tries to say things
but her words get tripped,
When she speaks with love my world gets
flipped,
It's in her lips,

It's in her smile, though it's been a while,
She's the one I'd walk with, miles,
She wears kindness as her style,
Wow, it's in her smile,

It's in her soul but does she even know?
Only for her I can give my all,
I'll be there to catch before she even falls,
But it's in her soul

It's in her fingertips,
She holds my hand,
My body shivers and then she tightens the
grip,
I never really thought but we sailed this ship,
It's in her fingertips,

It's in her hair, I wish she was here,
I wonder the way she does things with care,
She stole my heart and I have got no spare,
I wanted it back but then left it there,
It's in her hair,

She's love because she's kind,
I try to walk away but she makes me change
my mind,
We go on and off, we go forward and then we
push the rewind,
She's kind, she's so kind.

Move on babygirl, no soul is
meant to be undesired.

You are my " finally" after a long tired day.

You may feel bad for your good heart for a while but remember footprints of the kindness never wash away with time.

How beautiful people look with
all their walls down.

She hides her wings beneath her bones but I know she has come definitely from the city of gods.

Smiling lips and laughing tears, That's
what I see in all our good years.

Oh dear! Let the love save you this time.

Hey precious, make sure you bloom to the fullest in your own garden of love.

Let kindness lead your way and all your wars will be over eventually.

All the poets are drunk,
Some on the love, some on the pain,
Some on the words, some on the rain.

I love the way she admits openly that
she's having an affair with the kindness.

But they don't know that you know,
that I'm not gonna leave,
If love is spelled,
I am 'L' you are my 'E'.

And the way she loves god
makes him fall for her more.

Remind her everyday how beautiful
she is, even in her 80s.

But when the tides hit the shore, do
they promise they'll come back?

Don't leave her like a last drop of whiskey in the club full of strangers.

Oh! let my words warm you, I heard you've been cold since ages.

Try to touch the roots of her scars
and then you'll know her strength.

Kind, sweetheart, you make me kind.

And when my daughter will ask
"dad, what does mommy do?
I'll say "she creates magic as she created you".

You're the happiness adhered
to my chaotic soul.

She sets me free, so beautifully and wildly.

And so often we forget that loving them is one thing and keeping them is different.

Love her to the point where her eyes
can tell the happiness of her soul.

The universe gets drunk over one sip of her madness, I can't believe you still wonder how I became a poet.

If it puts you into might be's or
maybe's, don't go for it.

Out of all the reasons for what I loved her,
her fu*king smile has been my favourite.

There are countless memories
we still owe each other.

Last night I tripped over my thoughts and the ink spilled all over me and the words laughed as they knew it was you that I was thinking about.

I hope our stubborness of not giving
up on each other may never die.

What really keeps me going is the
transparency of her heart.

There are places in me I've never been at, but you have.

Your traces at my fingertips still have
the scent of our good old times.

Don't confuse bitter words with bitter hearts for I have seen kindness in the hearts that speak the most bitter words.

She plays wild, in wild, barefoot,
her own music where all you
could hear is her soul's voice.

My life got an empty pages, it seems like you're the poetry who'd fit in.

Never ever leave them with
the chaos undefined.

You're my light at the end of the tunnel.

If only she knew that her love makes me dance over the sea and ride upon the wind.

And people who ask "why you're still holding on to the love? are the people who will never understand that no matter how much we hate the sun in the noon but we always stop to admire the sunset.

Breathe in the love that you've
been breathing out lately.

She's my oasis in the desert full of chaos.

Crave them, even when they're yours.

I'll marry her soul in the middle of the sky and I believe all the stars will ablaze when she'll say "I do".

Kindness is the outfit that fits over almost
every soul, you just gotta be brave
enough to wear it all the time.

Be the reason that they start
wishing for more years of life.

Darling, let your soul fly high in the skies of faith and believe me hopes will follow.

Believe me or not but we all can be great architectures when it comes to decorate our souls but only if we choose to be.

They were calling her sweet so I kissed her, you know, I don't trust people.

Don't be too absorbed by the feeling of being loved that you almost forget that even too much is painful in the end sometimes.

And she has always been inspired by the other people I wonder if she has ever looked at the warrior in the mirror.

She finds peace in her solace just like
a coconut tree on the beach alone.

And our vibes match just like
the chords to a song.

I love the way she heard the
words I didn't even say.

# *Fairytale*

While telling our story they'll start
with " once upon a time"

In this ocean of lies, I am trying to find my way back to the truth, to you, my only truth.

Too many sunsets tell this story
that every nemo gets his dory.

If you really want to sit close to her fire then you must be strong enough to fire up all her flames.

The enough in her is enough for me

Lock me in the heaven but I will still
be impatient if you aren't there.

And the spaces between our fingers remind me of how much helpless we are sometimes.

She never really waits for her knight
in shining armor as she's strong
enough to kill the dragon alone.

She carries my words against her skin, inside
her heart, right where they should be.

All she asks for is some comfort,
some rain and whole lot of love.

Of what use is the beauty that
doesn't know kindness?

I adore all those butterflies which show
up when my skin touches yours.

Be like flowers, not afraid of being plucked,
Being broken but always wishing for smiles.

At any moment, doesn't matter what you think, the universe makes every single thing correspond to your energy.

Every now and then, you'll get the feeling of being invincible at something and exactly in those moments you're the most vulnerable.

No matter how dark the night is, she always faces it like a stubborn sun that never fails to come out.

And she lays herself these days with not a single notion in her mind. Away from the fire of her past, fireproof, so blithely.

Leave it if it hurts, why trying to swim in a pond when there's an ocean to surf?

And the way she merges her pain into her power, she can make strength come to her door asking for strength.

And he adores her scars like
they're Fu*king stars

If the whole world was dancing and riding over unicorns with rainbows all over their heads, I'd still look into your eyes and tell lie that they aren't beautiful.

Love cannot be measured by the quantity of years you spent with them but by the quality of moments where their souls laughed to the ears.

With her glittering eyes, she looked to the stars and asked " aren't they beautiful? I looked into her eyes, smiled and asked myself the same.

When she was born, universe asked
the god "what you just created?
God smiled and whispered " happiness"

Under the other side of the sky, we belong to each other. Believe me.

Beneath her bones, she holds the
fire to keep the universe alive.

And when her soul smiles, the universe smiles back.

I thought there was nothing else beautiful than her smile until I looked into her star lit eyes.

Perfect to all is a perfect to none,
darling, flaws are beautiful.

And what makes me wonder is that if she deserves the poetry or poetry deserves her?

And the way she calmed my fire of the past, I knew I have met healing.

My soul sparkles and my chaos laugh out loud, so the universe leaves me with no reason but to believe that she is god sent.

She's a soul of mixed signals but
all coming out of kindness.

Right love will show you the magic
that the universe has been hiding.

Call it love when your heart realises they're around before your eyes do.

Find the ones who make you
believe that the heaven is real

I could write thousands of poems about her and I guess they still won't be enough to describe the magic that she holds.

It took her years to learn that
self love is the key.

I wish it's only my heart that becomes home for the madness that she carries.

And everytime when I look at her, my mind says " oh fool, you're so full of luck"

I love the heaven, you, and
the skies in between.

The butterflies in the stomach might be the demons striving to eat your soul. Be careful, babygirl.

It will be a different story if somehow
we remember that love brings
life, life doesn't bring love.

Your love makes me write everyday.
Believe me I am not a poet from within.

She's the spring to my soul flowers.

Her fierce love cuts me like a sword and I
stand still just to see her smile afterwards.

I wonder how far less beautiful the world of beauty would be only if she didn't exist.

The fire in you nourishes the fire in me.
Together we can forge a madness
that people can't take eyes off of.

Why keeping your stars hidden darling?
Did any human born just to stay alive?

She's so good,
As good as the rainbows,
As the flowers,
As the rain,
As the god,
She's good.

Emerged out of love, she
keeps the souls alive,
what can I say about her, she
brings life to my life.

# About the author

Karanjodh Singh was born and raised in Punjab, India and he moved to US after his bachelors. After his high school, he realised that he's a bookworm. So he kept on jumping from one book to another until he decided to write one of his own. He has a big nose and forehead for no good reason.

When not writing you can find him wandering in the nature parks, talking to dogs, or watching F.R.I.E.N.D.S or soccer on Sunday afternoons. Above all, he believes that kindness is the cure to all the wars.

# *Acknowledgements*

I want to thank you

Tania Bawa

Ekamjot kaur

Kuljeet kaur

Shruti sharma

Saumya jain

Daisy kalsi ( monicaaa )

Yogesh sagar

Barkat singh

Saurav kumar

Neegam Nain

Temwanani Nyasulu

And all my classmates, friends, seniors and teachers that made me see this sparkle I never knew I had. And also a big Thank you to Writersrepublic for turning my dream into a reality. Much love, take care.

—*karanjodh*

CPSIA information can be obtained
at www.ICGtesting.com
Printed in the USA
LVHW091509290121
677776LV00001B/3